SPIDERS!

A MY INCREDIBLE WORLD PICTURE BOOK

MY INCREDIBLE WORLD

Photo Credits:
Cover. Julian Göbel, available at https://unsplash.com/photos/Geu9kXvorzA
Page 1. Krzysztof Niewolny, available at https://unsplash.com/photos/MltCHTby8kg
Page 2. Gary Yost, available at https://unsplash.com/photos/LQX23a6An9A
Page 3. David Clode, https://unsplash.com/photos/6RE5Ilcj-QU
Page 4. Juan Pablo Mascanfroni, available at https://unsplash.com/photos/csxW2avUgmM
Page 5. James Wainscoat, available at https://unsplash.com/photos/F_p4sI8Vj0Q
Page 6. Germán Rodríguez, available at https://unsplash.com/photos/soyjfd_DDXw
Page 7. Fabian Michel, available at https://unsplash.com/photos/NcH5I25xuX4
Page 8. Егор Камелев, available at https://unsplash.com/photos/e8uB23q9yl8
Page 9. Егор Камелев, available at https://unsplash.com/photos/R5MgBBhrm4Q
Page 10. Timothy Dykes, available at https://unsplash.com/photos/eW59sn3qJVc
Page 11. Julian Schultz, available at https://unsplash.com/photos/TWmblnGmmbM
Page 12. Stephen Hocking, available at https://unsplash.com/photos/obANw0UNzBc
Page 13. Robert Thiemann, available at https://unsplash.com/photos/tA3W6yzs1-s
Page 14. Timothy Dykes, available at https://unsplash.com/photos/LSMlc4Q1LV8
Page 15. Pietro De Grandi, available at https://unsplash.com/photos/_Ka47lOaWsw
Page 16. Victoria Naumenko, available at https://unsplash.com/photos/f0y72o-PKHo
Page 17. Timothy Dykes, available at https://unsplash.com/photos/HUnGjn5ChPg
Page 18. Andy Holmes, available at https://unsplash.com/photos/xgcP78yRcO4
Page 19. Alexandre Debiève, available at https://unsplash.com/photos/UtcgLhpi-ME
Page 20. Bankim Desai, available at https://unsplash.com/photos/Zu_Zh73mPYQ
Page 21. Juan Pablo Mascanfroni, available at https://unsplash.com/photos/Zwpu_9_PuIQ
Page 22. Timothy Dykes, available at https://unsplash.com/photos/u0VVgs8YjYI

Spiders are found in habitats
all over the world!

There are over 45,000 known
species of spiders!

Spiders can be many colors, including black, yellow, red, green, and even blue!

Spiders are not insects,
they are **arachnids**.

Most spiders spin webs to catch insects to eat, but others pounce on their prey!

Spider web silk is stonger
than steel for its weight!

It takes around 30 to 60 minutes for a spider to spin a web.

Spiders usually have 8 eyes,
but some have up to 12!

Spiders can see ultraviolet colors that humans can't see!

The smallest spider species is
0.4 millimeters - too small to see
without a magnifying glass!

The biggest species has a
leg span of up to one foot!

Female spiders can lay up to 3,000 eggs at one time!

Baby spiders are called **spiderlings**.

Jumping spiders can jump
up to 50 times their body length.

Spider blood is blue!

Some tarantulas can fling tiny
hairs at predators as a defense!

Some spiders sing and dance
to attract a mate.

Spiders usually live about
2 years, but some live up to 20!

Even though spiders have venom, most are harmless to humans!

Spiders are important because they keep insect populations in check.

Spiders eat more insects than
bats and birds combined!

Spiders are incredible!

Made in the USA
Las Vegas, NV
28 October 2024

10622902R00017